TEXT: **Bill Harris**

CAPTIONS: **Susan Hazen-Hammond**

PHOTOGRAPHY: **Eduardo Fuss**

DESIGN: **Teddy Hartshorn**

DIRECTOR OF PRODUCTION: **Gerald Hughes**

CLB 3241
© 1993 CLB Publishing, Godalming, Surrey, England.
All rights reserved.
This 1993 edition published by Crescent Books,
distributed by Outlet Book Company, Inc., a Random House Company,
40 Engelhard Avenue, Avenel, New Jersey 07001.
Random House
New York • Toronto • London • Sydney • Auckland
Printed and bound in Malaysia.
ISBN: 0 517 10055 X
8 7 6 5 4 3 2 1

SOUTHWEST INDIANS

A Photographic Journey

Text by
BILL HARRIS

Photography by
EDUARDO FUSS

CRESCENT BOOKS
NEW YORK • AVENEL, NEW JERSEY

The problem may be that all the writers were on the other side. When the white man came into their midst, the Native Americans relied on oral tradition to record their side of the story, and it was generally lost to anyone out of earshot. The Europeans, on the other hand, often had somebody nearby taking notes, keeping diaries, writing official reports, and most of what we know about the history of the first inhabitants of the Southwest is what we've read in their papers. But the Indian oral histories have been kept alive, and Americans are finally beginning to listen to them.

The new evidence still raises almost as many questions as it gives answers. One of the biggest obstacles Native Americans have had to overcome is their image as bloodthirsty savages, an image created by hundreds of 20th-century movies and thousands of 19th-century adventure novels. Even the accounts of the generals and soldiers who fought the Indians – and it seems every Anglo-American military man who could spell felt compelled to write his story – regularly refer to the red men as "hostiles," whose only pleasure was inflicting pain and suffering. But even if the white man today sees the Indians as peace-loving people who were driven to the only means at hand to protect their freedom, the tribal histories themselves reveal tales of atrocities by one tribe against another. Even today there is no love lost among the Hopi in Arizona for the Navajo who surround them and, they claim, are still making their lives miserable.

The truth, most likely, is that there is plenty of guilt to go around on all sides. But there is no question that although the Indians of the Southwest are the only Native Americans whose ancestral lands are still largely theirs, they have been denied their fair share of the "American Dream."

The earliest evidence of human life in the Southwest is butchering tools and other implements that have been dated back to approximately 38,000 BC. In southern New Mexico human palm prints have been found that date to about 26,000 BC. In about 9000 BC Southwest Indians were hunting woolly mammoths and mastodons. When the great prehistoric beasts became victims of a climate change that began creating a desert landscape, the original Americans followed them inland, but by about 6000 BC new people began arriving in what is now Arizona and decided to settle down. At first they hunted small game and augmented their diet with seeds, roots and berries, giving no thought to farming, but there is evidence at the site of one of their villages in Cochise County, Arizona, of tools for grinding seeds and roots for storage. Farming came later in the form of corn, which seems to have arrived in New Mexico from the South in about 4000 BC, and once the people were able to control their own food supply they began living together in villages. By 300 BC they had perfected the arts of basketry and had learned to make pottery, and were, to all intents and purposes, an emerging civilization following the same kinds of patterns that brought civilization to the ancient Near East.

Archaeologists divide the people who emerged from this Archaic Desert culture into three major groups: the Mogollon, named for the mountains of southern Arizona and New Mexico; the Hohokam, for a Pima word meaning "those who have gone away"; and the Anasazi, a Navajo word meaning "Old Ones." The Mogollon lived in the high mountains and built their houses in pits roofed over with logs and brush, usually in communities of twenty or more. Eventually, all of the pits had holes in the floor to contain a cooking fire, and in time the Mogollon people developed bows and arrows that replaced spears for hunting small game. The Hohokam, who also lived in holes in the ground, inhabited the Arizona desert, which they made bloom with squash and corn by digging canals to carry water from the rivers to their fields. Essentially, both groups were farmers and are believed to be the first agricultural societies in North America. However, although they became quite skilled at producing their own food – traditionally the essential first step to becoming civilized – their culture was eventually overshadowed by the Anasazi who lived to their north.

When they first arrived in the Southwest, probably from Mexico, the Anasazi hadn't yet figured out how to make pottery, and although they knew the rudiments of farming they had no notion of how to coax good yields from the soil. They hadn't mastered the art of building, either, and found shelter in shallow caves, under piles of brush, or in rudimentary pit houses. But although we might consider them primitive, they were obviously both willing to learn and inventive in their own right. The Anasazi were highly accomplished basket makers and developed tightly woven baskets that could hold water. Some of these were used for cooking, using heated stones which were dropped into the basket to boil the water. The same weaving skills also helped them construct huge nets to catch small game at the mouths of canyons. Although the people to the south were already using bows and arrows the Anasazi didn't seem to know about them in the earliest period. They gradually learned about the more sophisticated hunting weapons as well as better farming techniques by watching their neighbors, and their forays also gave them the idea of placing roofs over pits to make more comfortable houses. In time they improved on the idea, with such innovations as lining the floors and walls with stone slabs and piling stones in front of the fire pits to prevent sudden flare-ups, a problem their neighbors never solved.

Most of what is known about the Anasazi began coming to light in the 1890s, when ruins of their villages and cities were discovered across the Southwest. In general, a picture emerged of the oldest of the Old Ones as a comparatively backward people, who were given the name "Basketmakers." Over time they developed into a much more advanced culture that not only created fine pottery and used bows and arrows, but lived in above-ground houses. The fact that the newer Pueblo cities often existed where Basketmaker villages once stood gave rise to the theory that invaders had swept down from the North and wiped out the culture they found. The idea was all the more believable because Basketmaker burial sites indicated that they had been a people with narrow, elongated skulls, while the Pueblo-builders had broad, round heads. It wasn't until the 1940s that archaeologists and anthropologists put their heads together and put the theory to rest by looking beyond what had seemed obvious. The scientists found evidence that, over the centuries, Basketmaker mothers placed their babies in cradles made of sticks tied together to form a flexible bed, but such a thing didn't seem too important in the scheme of things. But they also knew that around the beginning of the 8th century, the women began to place boards under the heads of their newborns in a conscious effort to flatten the backs of their skulls, a custom that had been prevalent in South America for hundreds of years, and was still practiced by the Pueblo Indians, the descendants of the Anasazi, when the Spanish arrived. The flattening process caused the front of the babies' skulls to broaden, and eventually the entire race looked dramatically different from its ancestors. Armed with the new evidence, scientists concluded that there hadn't been an invasion after all, just a change in fashion. But a revolution of thought was clearly under way.

The great change began around AD 700, when the Old Ones started building their above-ground houses. At first, they simply drove poles into the ground and, after binding them together with reeds, covered them with layers of mud. The walls surrounded traditional pit houses, but it was a step up, and once the Anasazi learned how to build straight walls and put roofs over them, the pits lost their function as living quarters. At the same time, they began linking their rectangular houses together and soon began substituting stones for the reeds between the poles to make stronger walls. Before long the wooden poles themselves disappeared except for a few to support the roof, which was still made the old-fashioned way of logs lashed together with reeds and plastered with mud. Over time they learned to cut sandstone into blocks, and in many regions the adobe mud became a binding material rather than the main construction element, and the next logical step was to use the stronger walls to support a second story. By AD 1000 nearly all the Anasazi villages were rows of two-story stone buildings, and the only use the people had for the old pit house was a below-ground structure, the common denominator of all Pueblo Indian people, that served as both a religious and social center, known to their descendants as the *kiva*.

Ruins of more than a dozen major villages line Chaco Canyon, New Mexico, and one of the most fascinating of them is Pueblo Bonito, a collection of more than 800 apartments, some in stacks five stories high, that was once home to more than 1,200 people and was, until the middle of the 19th century, the largest apartment building in the world. Construction began in about AD 900, and archaeologists speculate that after a century and a half new residents arrived and expanded its size with improved construction techniques. Probably the original inhabitants didn't leave, but moved into less desirable rooms in the back of the village, creating a kind of ghetto where they continued to live in the same old familiar way. Then construction, which had been continuous from the beginning, suddenly stopped, and the new inhabitants began to leave. The exodus seems to have lasted for almost thirty years, but apparently the original people stayed on for many more years. No one knows why. The ones who stayed walled up the buildings outer doors which the new builders had created, and even sealed off the gate in the wall around the village. Some evidence suggests that Pueblo Bonito may have been under siege by an invading enemy. But archaelogists have a different theory.

Dating of most of the ruins is done by a process known as dendrochronology, the counting of tree rings. The process was developed early in the 1900s by Dr. Andrew E. Douglass, who studied cross-sections of pine trees growing in Arizona, looking for clues to climate cycles. Armed with the knowledge that a tree adds a growth band each year and in a dry desert climate the width of the band was determined by the amount of rainfall in a given year, Dr. Douglass was able to chart weather patterns back more than 600 years, as well as accurately to date any tree that began growing after the start of the 14th century. Then, using samples taken from the wooden roof beams at several pueblo ruins, he was able to concoct a series of what he called "floating chronologies" that eventually, through painstaking comparisons, reached back to AD 11. He was able to pinpoint the date with amazing accuracy. His work made dating ancient Pueblo Indian villages a precise science, but his field was astronomy not archaeology, and just as important as knowing when the pueblos were built, he also provided a reliable record of the weather for every season almost from the beginning of the Christian era. And according to the weather reports of the tree rings, the decade of the 1090s, when people began moving out of Chaco Canyon, was a period of devastating droughts.

Without water, the Anasazi obviously faced starvation, but even if the weather hadn't changed, they'd probably have been doomed anyway. The Old Ones had systematically ruined their own environment. The canyon was filled with thick forests before they began building their villages, but over time they cut down all the trees both to create farmland and to provide building material. As the root systems died, there was nothing to hold the topsoil in place or to hold back the spring floods, and eventually the canyon that had supported a population in the thousands was filled with ghost towns. No one knows where the people went, but the best guess is that they moved on to build the pueblo at Aztec, New Mexico, about sixty miles away. The new city was built in the short space of about a dozen years, beginning in 1110, and the builders apparently followed a careful plan. Then, by the end of the century, the pueblo was suddenly and completely abandoned. The people who built it simply disappeared without trace and for no apparent reason. Their city stood empty for a hundred years until it was taken over and remodeled by wanderers from the North.

The newcomers were also Anasazi, and the land they came from, Mesa Verde, is often regarded as the true homeland of the Old Ones. In the surrounding territory it is still possible to trace the full history of their architecture, from primitive pit houses to the earliest walled structures, all the way to the multi-storied stone buildings that evolved over a period of seven centuries. A tour of the area leads to former farms and villages on the tops of mesas, which historians say were abandoned at about the same time as Chaco Canyon, and to the fortified cities that replaced them. It is those cities, the third stage of Anasazi architecture, that capture the imagination today, because they are precariously perched on the sides of cliffs, like castles in the air.

It seems probable that they were built in response to raids by hostile neighbors for the cliff dwellings were as impregnable as any medieval castle in Europe. Most of them were built in shallow caves protected from above by overhanging rocks and from below by high canyon walls. In every case, they were reached by narrow trails that were easily defended, and the Anasazi seem to have created a perfect way to secure themselves against the most determined marauders. But the idea had a fatal flaw. There was no way to grow food on the rocky shelves and very few of them had their own water supply. It was necessary for the men to climb up to the mesas or down into the valleys to tend their crops, and for the women to make repeated trips for water. There are no signs of any actual warfare in the Mesa Verde region, but it is possible that the enemies of the Anasazi picked them off one at a time whenever they left the security of the pueblo. They may also have been victims of another devastating drought that lasted almost twenty-five years. Whatever the reason, by 1300 all the cliff dwellers had gone from Mesa Verde, even though their civilization had reached a kind of Golden Age there, both in terms of accomplishment and security. In spite of the drought, there is evidence that their food storage bins were well filled, and there are also signs in their artistry that the Anasazi lived rich, full lives during their three centuries as cliff-dwellers. For some reason, however, they felt compelled to wander off. The Old Ones moved east and south and built new pueblos in the Rio Grande valley. Their language and customs are still kept alive by their descendants and heirs: the Pueblo tribes of the Rio Grande valley and other parts of New Mexico and the pueblo-building Hopi in Arizona.

According to a Hopi tradition, a stranger arrived one day at one of their villages looking for food. He was followed soon after by others who were also hungry, and all were fed and provided with shelter. The Hopi say they also taught the strangers how to grow crops and weave cotton, but that they got very little in return. The barbarians had no legends to share, nor any rituals of their own, and they never stopped eating until all the food was gone. Before long they began stealing corn, and that led to a declaration of war. The Hopis were able to fight off their new enemy and the thieving stopped for a time, but peace had disappeared from the land of the Anasazi. The Hopis called the enemy Tuvasuh, "head-pounders," because of their terrifying skill with stone axes. They called themselves Dineh, "The People," but we call them Navajo.

The Navajo and their close relatives, the Apache, arrived in the Southwest at least six hundred years ago. Their language was quite different, related to the speech of tribes living in the Pacific Northwest, and was quite unlike any tongue understood for a thousand miles around. They learned new skills and picked up some of the customs of the people who had become their neighbors, but they seem to have had no stomach for settling down on farms. They were a race of semi-nomadic farmers who lived in sod houses in the cold months; the rest of the year they preferred hogans, simple timber frames covered with mud or sod, that were easy to move, and they didn't seem to think that adobe pueblo houses were at all practical.

But if the newcomers from the North were misunderstood, feared and despised because they were different, the next wave of strangers who became the true enemies of all Indians were anticipated as saviors by a host of ancient legends. The Hopi believed that a white god called Pahána would eventually come to live among them, and the Navajo believed that the pale-skinned Klehonoai, their god of the moon, would one day take on an earthly form. Further south, the Mayans believed in the return of the white-bearded god Kukulcan, and the Aztec priests had predicted that their god of civilization,

Quetzalcoatl, would bring new light back to earth in the year their calendar named Ce Acatl and ours translates as 1519. The exact date turned out to be April 22, 1519, but the white man who appeared in the court of the Emperor Montezuma that day was no god. He was the Spanish conquistador Hernando Cortés, and the result of his appearance was a total disaster for the Aztecs. The Hopi astrologers had also predicted that their god Pahána would return during the same year, but twenty years passed before a white man appeared among the Pueblo Indians.

After the Spanish conquered Mexico, Francisco Vásquez de Coronado led an expedition to the North in search of the fabled seven cities of Cibola, where the Spaniards had been told they'd find a fabulous fortune in gold and precious stones. Finding nothing more than the adobe pueblos of the Zuni, which they looted, Coronado sent Pedro de Tovar with a small force to check out rumors of more cities farther north. They hadn't gone far when a delegation of Hopis appeared in their camp, convinced that Pahána had returned. They drew a line of sacred cornmeal across the path, but the Spaniards took it as a challenge rather than the symbolic gesture of welcome it was, and immediately attacked. The Hopi should have got the message then and there, but instead they invited Tovar to their village. He was met by the assembled clan chiefs, one of whom extended his hand palm upward knowing that the true Pahána would respond by extending his hand palm down in an ancient form of what modern kids call a "high five." Instead, the Spaniard took it as a form of begging and dropped a gift into the chief's hand. Tovar had failed the second test, but still the Hopis persisted and called for a council of peace, offering to merge their culture, religion and lands with the white men. Tovar was noncommittal, and in the absence of gold among the Hopis he decided he had already given them more time than they were worth and moved on.

The Coronado expedition was preceded in 1539 by a group intended to pacify the Indians and to determine the best route to follow to the golden cities. The former was the job of Fray Marcos de Niza, a Franciscan missionary, and the scouting was entrusted to a man known as Estevan, a Moor, who may have been black and who had migrated to the New World from Spain. Estevan had been a member of a group of shipwrecked sailors, led by Alvar Nuñez Cabeza de Vaca, who walked across Texas and perhaps southern New Mexico a few years earlier. During his journey he learned some of the secrets of the Indian medicine men. He had acquired a sacred rattle, the outward sign of such knowledge, and he had also adopted a flamboyant personal style that must have been the envy of every medicine man he ever met. He had a fondness for brightly colored beads and was decked out in feathers and bells; his constant companions were a pair of greyhounds which were always at his side, and he was followed by a harem of Indian women. His sacred rattle preceded him, and when he arrived in a village it served as his entrée to the highest councils, where he was able to describe the men who were following in glowing terms. But his magic didn't impress the Zunis. When Estevan reached the first of their cities, he was dismayed to find that there were two strikes against him. First of all, the rattle that was his symbol of authority was covered with markings of southern tribes the Zunis regarded as their enemies, and second, the reputation of the white man had gone ahead of him. Although Estevan wasn't Spanish, it didn't matter and he was executed along with most of the Indians who had come with him. The friar, who preferred to follow the Moor rather than accompany him, escaped the wrath of the Zuni and lived to accompany Coronado himself on his search for gold in the Southwest the following year.

None of the tribes was overjoyed to see them come, and the lack of gold didn't make Coronado very happy, either. He vented his frustration by attacking the settlements, and the Indians gave as good as they got. However, the Spaniards hadn't come all this way to make war. It was riches they were after and, realizing that, the Pueblo people gulled them into believing that they'd find fabulous treasure if they'd just keep on moving. The strategy worked, but not because the Pueblo elders were so convincing. Coronado headed for the Great Plains after talking with a Plains Indian man who was a slave at Pecos Pueblo. This man, called El Turco by the Spaniards because he looked like a Turk, said that he had come from a place called Quivira, where the people ate from dishes of pure gold and where the buildings were studded with precious stones. He agreed to guide them there, but after weeks of marching, Coronado began to suspect he had been tricked and had El Turco tortured until he admitted that he had lied. In spite of the confession, however, the Spaniards still believed in the existence of Quivira and kept on marching until they found El Turco's city, but not a trace of gold, in what is now Kansas. El Turco was executed for his perfidy and Coronado returned to Mexico, where he was stripped of his rank and discredited as a failure. With that the Spanish lost interest in the land of the Pueblos, and the tribes of the Southwest were safe from any further expeditions for another forty years.

The next invasion, in 1581, was a march to save souls rather than to search for riches, and although the Christian missionaries penetrated deep into Zuni territory in modern New Mexico, they were killed for their trouble, an event that eventually spelled trouble for the Indians. Soldiers followed the friars, and when they reached Arizona they found deposits of gold and silver which prompted them to begin lobbying the Spanish crown for a charter to colonize the area. The winner of the royal favor was Juan de Oñate, who established himself in New Mexico in 1598, and, after securing promises from the local chiefs to welcome the Spaniards in peace, sent word to Mexico that a new colony was open for business. In the meantime he took an extended trip to explore his new domain, and when he returned to his headquarters he found it almost deserted. Some of the settlers returned, but by 1610 Oñate, who failed to find the gold and silver deposits that lay all around the Southwest, was ordered home to Mexico. But if they had found no riches worth the effort, there were still souls to save, and by 1680 there were about 3,500 Spanish settlers in Pueblo country, and more than 60,000 natives had agreed to accept the white man's god. At least they gave lip service to Christian belief, but they missed the old gods who had sustained them and their ancestors, and deeply resented the Spanish penchant for making slaves of them.

The Spaniards had few illusions about the situation. There had been enough uprisings to tell them that they were in danger, but they hoped that the evil they faced was simple witchcraft, and they fought back with hangings and the torture of suspected witches. One of the accused was Popé, the medicine man of San Juan Pueblo. He escaped hanging, but after a severe whipping and imprisonment, he began nursing a smoldering hate for the Christians, which he spread throughout the pueblo villages. He also secretly organized a plot for rebellion, which erupted simultaneously in dozens of Indian pueblos in August 1680. Priests were slaughtered in front of their altars as they were saying morning Mass, and settlers were killed in the streets. Survivors huddled inside the government buildings at Santa Fe. During the nine-day siege that followed, the church and convent were destroyed and the water supply cut, and the Indians might have succeeded in killing everyone inside if the commander of the garrison hadn't ordered his soldiers into what seemed a suicide charge against the invaders. When it was over they had killed three hundred Indians, and those who survived melted away. The Pueblo villages also emptied as the people fled for their lives. But the expected vengeance never came. Four hundred Spaniards had died, and the Spanish survivors of the Pueblo uprising began walking south. They didn't stop until they reached what is now El Paso, Texas, and New Mexico was once again free of outsiders. But it wasn't long before the people had a new master. Popé declared himself king of all the Pueblo Indians, a concept that had never been part of Indian life. Dictator would probably be a better word, because anyone who opposed him was put to death. But he had more opponents than he could deal with and before long the Pueblos were at war with one another.

When the Spanish tried to return in 1681, they found many of the villages destroyed and many more deserted, and before long, faced with the prospect of fighting Popé's rebels, they withdrew again, leaving the natives to fight among themselves. But Indian rule was short-lived. In 1692, a new and stronger Spanish army led by Don Diego de Vargas arrived in Santa Fe and took possession of it from its Indian defenders, who had obviously had enough after a dozen years of civil war and repeated raids by hostile mounted tribes from the North. Popé was dead by then and his successor, a powerful chief named Tupatú, pledged his allegiance to the Spanish king, and he and Vargas began a tour of the pueblos, each of which confirmed the pledge. But when Vargas returned to Santa Fe with settlers in 1693 it was occupied by Indian warriors, who had to be forced out. When the day-long siege was over he imprisoned the rebels and settled down to rebuilding the Spanish colony, believing that Tupatú's promise had been kept. But the following year Vargas made another tour of the pueblos, and he found open hostility that forced him to begin systematically reconquering them one at a time.

The Hopi were the last holdouts. They had been badly treated by the early waves of missionaries, and when new padres arrived to reconvert the people of the Awatobi pueblo in 1700, the other pueblos decided to nip the idea in the bud by destroying the town and everyone in it. They were completely successful, and the message of the massacre kept Christianity out of the Hopi pueblos for another century. Apart from the un-Christian behavior of the first missionaries, the Hopi had given up on the new religion because, after they stopped honoring the old gods, the rains stopped, crops failed and famine forced many whole clans to move. When a few of the survivors gathered to recreate the traditional ceremonies the rains miraculously returned, and they had what they saw as proof that their own gods were the more powerful. But in 1776 the gods failed the Hopi. There was no rain for three years and plague began to decimate the pueblos. By 1780, their population, which had been estimated to have been about seventy-five hundred, was reduced to less than eight hundred. Disease also took its toll among the other tribes and more than five thousand died in the Southwest in the same year. The drought also brought out the worst in the nomadic tribes who had horses by then, and they regularly swept down on the Pueblo Indian villages in search of the food they knew was stored inside.

The raids by Navajo and Apache warriors continued well into the 19th century. In an earlier time, the Pueblo peoples would simply have abandoned their homes and moved on, but the Spanish had appropriated the best sites to the south and the tribes they wanted to escape from had them blocked to the north. There was nothing left to do but stay and hope for the best, but things were about to get worse. A new kind of white man was beginning to arrive, and nothing would be the same again for any of the Indians of the Southwest.

The Spanish had lost control of the area to the Mexicans in 1821, and New Mexico changed rapidly as Anglo-Americans began arriving along the Santa Fe Trail. Twenty-five years later the United States went to war with Mexico, and on August 18, 1846 the American flag was hoisted over Santa Fe. Two years later, the Southwest officially became U.S. territory and the Pueblo Indians became wards of the Department of Indian Affairs, representing the Great White Father nearly two thousand miles away in a place called Washington, DC. The Pueblo tribes had no desire for war, which had never been part of their way of life, and although they had no reason to trust any white man, they accepted their new masters. At least there was hope that they might give the Navajo and Apache something new to think about.

But in the meantime, none of them knew very much about the history of these new white men and how events of earlier decades, hundreds of miles away, would affect them. Not long after the Spanish arrived in the Southwest, immigrants from England began establishing colonies on North America's East Coast, beginning a pattern of pushing the Native Americans inexorably westward. In 1825, the so-called Five Civilized Tribes – the Cherokee, Choctaw, Chickasaw, Creek and Seminole – whose land was coveted for expanding cotton plantations, were asked to move west into the Oklahoma Territory. It took fifteen years before the move was actually made, and the time was used to rearrange the native peoples already there, making the Wichita, Osage, Comanche and Kiowa ready-made enemies when the Eastern tribes finally arrived on the scene. Army troops accompanied them to keep everybody apart and, hopefully, at peace, and the scheme worked. But the plan also prevented white Americans from settling that portion of the West. Some settled in the Mexican territory of Texas, but it was only a matter of time before they moved deeper into the Southwest, and the catalyst that lured them was what the Spanish had been trying to find for three hundred years: there was gold in the American West.

The most popular route to the California gold fields was across the Oregon Trail far to the north, but word of cholera and hostile plains tribes made many thousands choose the Santa Fe Trail and others across the Southwest. Although they were just passing through, and provided the Indians with an opportunity to sell them supplies, many came back to stay, and the American population of the Southwest mushroomed. As far as the Native Americans were concerned, the Gold Rush and its aftermath was, in the words of a contemporary diarist, " … fraught with greater evil for them than any other one event in the history of America, except the discovery of America itself."

Although there were many confrontations between white man and red, possibly the one that had the most far-reaching effects happened in 1851, when the Chiricahua Apache the Spanish called Mangas Coloradas, "Red Sleeves," was ambushed and savagely beaten by a band of gold prospectors who thought he was planning to kill them. The incident filled him with hate for all whites. He led his warriors all over Arizona and New Mexico, and even into Texas, on a rampage of vengeance and slow death, and at home he convinced the other Apache chiefs that they should follow his lead. Among them was a man said to be his brother-in-law or his son-in-law, the Chiricahua leader Cochise. The Chiricahua Apaches had been considered a peaceful band, and Cochise himself had offered protection for a stagecoach line that crossed their tribal lands, but the peace was broken one day in 1860, when Apaches kidnapped a white boy and stole a herd of cattle. Assuming that the Chiricahuas were the perpetrators, a detachment of soldiers was sent to the stagecoach station, where they called for a council with Cochise. When the chief arrived they accused him of stealing the cattle and taking the boy, and they placed him and his men under arrest as hostages until they were returned. Cochise, who denied any knowledge of the affair, responded by running for freedom, although several of his warriors were left behind as prisoners. In the gunfight that followed, the soldiers were pinned down in the station corral, but one managed to slip away for help at almost the same time that the stagecoach from California arrived badly shot-up by Cochise's people.

By the time fresh infantry troops arrived in the area the Chiricahuas had made prisoners of several whites, who were taken out to the plain to meet them and to be offered in exchange for the Indian hostages. When the soldiers moved on without making a deal Cochise ordered his prisoners tortured to death, and the following day the whites retaliated by hanging six Indian braves. The war had begun. It would go on for twenty-five years at a cost of thousands of lives.

Six months after Cochise joined with Mangas Coloradas to extend the reign of terror, a new kind of terror was unleashed with the bombardment of Fort Sumter in South Carolina, and America was plunged into a civil war. The troops that had been sent to deal with the Indians of the Southwest were recalled, and the Apache, who knew nothing of the white man's war, decided that the soldiers had retreated out of fear of them and began an unchecked rampage to drive all of the white men from their land. There wasn't much that the Union and the Confederacy could agree about, but in 1862 both sides decided that the Apache must be eliminated. The idea came first to Colonel John R. Baylor, the Confederate governor of Arizona, who formally petitioned President Jefferson Davis to issue an order for "the extermination of the grown Indians and making slaves of the children." Davis responded by firing Baylor, but on the Union side, General J.H. Carleton, who had led troops east from California to join the war but found a different sort of enemy when he reached New Mexico, got full support from Washington for a similar proposal. In the words of his general order to his troops: "The men are to be slain whenever and wherever they can be found. The women and children may be taken prisoners but, of course, they are not to be killed." The sparing of widows and orphans apparently took the stigma of genocide from the policy.

Most of Carleton's men were in the South, keeping the Apaches from raiding the wagon trains carrying gold eastward to support the war effort, and in New Mexico the job of tracking down the Indians fell to volunteers who had signed on to protect their land from the Confederates. They weren't organized, had few weapons and fewer horses, and in the absence of Confederates to fight, most considered their enlistments over. Even so, they were able to defeat a band of eastern Chiricahuas called Mescaleros in a few months, and the tribe was relocated to the Staked Plains of Southeastern New Mexico, in a place on the Little Pecos River the Spanish had called Bosque Redondo but the Americans called Fort Sumner. The key to their success was a colonel of the New Mexico Volunteers named Kit Carson, a man who chose not to follow Carleton's orders to the letter and was admittedly not much of a military man. But if Carson didn't know much about military tactics, he also didn't subscribe to the idea that the only good Indian was a dead Indian, and that, it turned out, was his secret weapon.

Once the Mescaleros were removed from the mountains, Carson turned his attention to the Navajo, but there were ten thousand of them spread out over millions of acres of territory, and he had about six hundred volunteers, more than half of whom had no horses. Such odds didn't stop Colonel Carson, however, and he issued an ultimatum ordering all Navajos to surrender. They had hardly stopped laughing when he issued a second proclamation among the other tribes offering bounties for horses, mules and sheep stolen from Navajo herds. Then he offered the Utes jobs as scouts with his army, and braves who considered the Navajo their worst enemy lined up to join the cause. The Zunis and Hopis were also enthusiastic supporters of these men who could give them guns to fight off the tribe that had been harassing their people for generations. The white man's war also gave the other tribes an opportunity to steal livestock from herds that had been built with animals stolen from them, and they smiled at the prospect of capturing women who could weave blankets for them. They all admired the Navajo blankets, but the prices the weavers charged put them out of reach. By going to war on the side of the white men, they'd have slaves to make all they wanted.

Faced with the prospect of fighting their hostile neighbors as well as the white men, the Navajos went into hiding in the high country, and when Carson went out to find them, he found nothing but abandoned fields and villages. So instead of killing Indians, he destroyed their crops. Over the summer months, many Navajos left their lands and dispersed, but it wasn't until fall that any began to surrender, and then in such small numbers it was quite evident that the Navajo will hadn't been broken. In January, as the snow was flying, Carson's men went into Canyon de Chelly, where they spotted Navajo warriors high above them, well out of reach. Then, as the soldiers were destroying the peach orchards in the canyon, small bands of Navajos began appearing to surrender and volunteering to convince their brothers to do the same. For the rest of the winter Carson retired to his headquarters at Fort Defiance and received surrendering Navajo families by the hundreds. His terms were simple. In exchange for a promise to stop raiding, they would be fed and clothed and in the spring removed to Fort Sumner, where the land was fertile and they'd be able to reconstruct their lives. In all, more than eight thousand Navajos took what their tribal histories call the Long Walk, three hundred miles on foot in the direction of the flat, treeless land that was to be their home.

The government's grand plan was to turn these people into farmers, but God seems to have had a different plan. The first year's crop was totally destroyed by a plague of caterpillars, and the following summer began with devastating floods and ended with severe drought, and again there was no food, except the meager, government-issued rations. The winter was no kinder, and before long the men were forced to walk as far as twenty miles for wood to keep their fires burning. When the crops failed in the second summer, more than a thousand captives escaped, including the Mescaleros, who headed back to their homeland. In a smallpox epidemic in 1865, more than two thousand prisoners died. By the third summer, when the crops failed again, the government did what governments do best, it conducted an investigation. Feeding all those Indians was getting expensive. The investigators decided the best thing to do was to move the Navajos again, and another investigation was launched to figure out where to send them. As the debate went on, the Navajos went on strike, refusing to plant another crop that would probably fail anyway, and the military began to panic. The solution was another treaty, this time a Navajo pledge never to fight again, not with other Indians, not with Mexicans, not with Americans. In return for the promise, they would be allowed to return to the countryside of their fathers, and on June 18, 1868, almost four years to the day from the time they left, the Navajos headed for home.

Their lives would be considerably changed, but during their years of captivity they had learned a great deal about the white man's ways, both good and bad, and of all the lessons they learned, the one that had the longest-lasting effect was that it was futile to fight back. A tribe with a long tradition of ruthless raiding and, yes, even head-pounding, became farmers and peaceful herders. They also learned a new skill that in their hands became a fine art unmatched by any other culture; the Navajo became silversmiths. In earlier times, the most prized booty from their raids on Mexican ranchers was bridles and saddles ornamented with silver, but since there was so much for the taking, it never occurred to the Navajo to attempt to make their own. According to their histories, when they were paid for their labor at Fort Sumner in silver dollars, they melted them down and taught themselves the art of working the metal into jewelry. The army's records of those same years indicate that they used the silver to forge metal tokens that were exchanged for daily meals, but either way, both sides agree that the Navajo skills as metalworkers began during their years in exile. And among the signs that they intended to settle down as good neighbors, they shared their new technology with the Pueblo tribes.

Washington's plan for the Navajos was to make them self-sufficient within ten years. It took more than three times that long and the credit for their climb from abject poverty seems to belong more to the Navajos than to the Great White Father, who was slow to move and often quite confused about what was best for these people he had asked to change their way of life completely. In the last thirty-one years of the 19th century, no less than fifteen different agents were sent in to take charge of the problem, and although they were frustrated by a lack of promised support from Washington, their annual reports were filled with admiration for their charges. "They are peaceful, well disposed, energetic, hardworking and industrious," said one. Another said that "The Navajo is by nature inclined to habits of industry ... his future improved condition is assured," but added that the future depended on government help, which had been promised but not forthcoming. But the Navajo qualities that so impressed the Indian agents served them well, and they were able to pull themselves up by their own bootstraps thanks to the new railroad that arrived in New Mexico in 1879. It brought entrepreneurial traders eager to buy Navajo wool, blankets and jewelry, which they paid for with food and tools and bolts of cloth. The traders, unlike the soldiers, learned the Navajo language and lived among the Indians as brothers, teaching them more about the white man's ways, possibly the most important of which was mass production techniques for turning out blankets faster. Women who once spun and died their own yarn began using commercial yarns with brighter colors than they had ever seen, and weavers who once took six months to create a blanket could now make four in the same length of time. Many responded to the new demand, and although the Navajo themselves had never used rugs, the traders encouraged them to make them, and a whole new industry was born. The traders guided them in creating new designs that would appeal to their customers back East and, in the process, the tribe became the most prosperous of all Native Americans at the time. By the turn of the century they owned more than 100,000 horses, not one of which had been stolen.

The situation was quite different among the Apaches. Early in 1863 soldiers captured Mangas Coloradas and, as he slept, sentries assigned to guard him stabbed him in the leg with a red-hot bayonet and then shot him as he stumbled to his feet. The seventy-year-old man had been trying to escape, they said. Next morning they decapitated him and sent his head off to New York for examination, a common practice in the 19th century when such "scientific study" was fashionable. After unceremoniously tossing his body into a gully the soldiers moved on. For the next several weeks they were never out of sight of Chiricahua warriors, who watched as their villages were destroyed and their livestock slaughtered. When they retaliated, Arizona was drenched in blood. Soldiers were occasionally able to trap the raiders, but Cochise took over as leader of the murdered Chief's followers, and vowed to kill one hundred whites for every Apache that died. Apaches seemed to be everywhere, and so elusive they might as well have been invisible. Within a year of its official designation as a Territory, Arizona was nearly deserted by white ranchers and miners. "The white people live on reservations," said one officer, "and the Indians occupy the country."

The army was enthusiastically supported in its policy of genocide by most of the Anglo-American citizens of New Mexico and Arizona, but Americans in other parts of the country were appalled. People who had championed the Abolitionist cause before and during the Civil War began turning their attention to the Indians of the Southwest, and finally, in 1869, Congress and President Ulysses S. Grant went to work to offer peace where war had failed, with plans for a new reservation system where the Native Americans could become self-supporting, educated and Christianized. The Peace Plan was hailed in the East, but to Arizonians and the military men in their area, it was viewed as a sellout. The Territorial governor, realizing that Washington wasn't going to send in fresh troops, encouraged citizens to kill every Indian they could find. The generals commanding the army there offered promotions to officers who brought in the greatest number of Apache scalps. The Apaches themselves, meanwhile, had no faith in Congress or the president, and the war escalated. By the beginning of 1870 General William T. Sherman wrote to his superiors that, "The best advice I can offer is to notify the settlers to withdraw and then to withdraw the troops and leave the country to the original inhabitants."

The Arizona Legislature countered with a report to Congress that said, "Probably but few countries on the face of the globe present greater natural resources inviting to immigration and capital than the Territory of Arizona." After pointing out that "every industry and enterprise has been paralyzed" by the Apaches, the document called for a reassessment of the peace plan and for help in eliminating "the implacable Apache."

The matter came to a head on the last day of April in 1871, when a band of vigilantes from Tucson led warriors of the Papago (O'odham) Tribe, old enemies of the Apaches, in a raid on the army's Camp Grant, where Apaches who had surrendered were being cared for. Without weapons to defend themselves, nearly 150 were slaughtered, of whom only eight were men. A score of able-bodied children were spared to become slaves of the Papagos. Washington ordered the inevitable investigations and promised that the massacre's perpetrators would be brought to justice. Among the early responses was the establishment of new Apache reservations, and by the end of the year more than four thousand had sought refuge in them. Naturally, the local citizens decided to attack again, but this time they were driven back by the soldiers, who were then castigated as "peace-lovers," with no respect for the "law-abiding citizens" who they were supposed to protect. In the meantime, a Tucson grand jury voted to indict the suspects in the Camp Grant massacre, but also included the charge that army officers were really at fault. In the five-day trial that followed, the jury took less than twenty minutes to acquit all 104 defendants.

But at the same time Apache raiding continued, and the national mood began to shift. Before long, President Grant agreed to send fresh troops into the Southwest and to give General George Crook carte blanche to "proceed with any measures he deems necessary." He began by issuing an ultimatum to the Apaches that any of them who were not on reservations by spring would be considered hostiles and either killed or captured as prisoners of war. In a kind of last gasp, the peace advocates managed to delay Crook's offensive and spring of 1872 found him talking with Apache leaders rather than killing them. But one who had no time for conversation was the Chiricahua, Cochise. He was far too busy raiding wagon trains and burning ranches, with losses of life and property among the worst the Southwest had seen.

In October 1872, Captain Thomas Jeffords, the only white man ever to become a blood brother of Cochise, convinced Cochise to agree to peace. But Cochise could speak only for his own warriors. There were other Apache bands and leaders to subdue. Crook's war began in earnest in November; more than six months after his ultimatum had expired, and he went into the field with the best-trained American army yet to go into battle against Indians. He also had the advantage of some forty Apache scouts attached to each company, free to fight their brothers in their own way with no constraints of military discipline. Thanks to the reliable scouts, Crook's army was able to strike terror into the Apaches, and by the end of the winter he confidently announced that he had ended a war that "has been waged since the days of Cortez." He wasn't quite right. The thousands of Apaches who surrendered were assigned to reservations and then generally forgotten. Faced with starvation and hostility from their white neighbors, most ran off in the direction of Mexico, where they joined others already there, including the Chiracahua under Cochise, and continued their raiding. At the same time, responding to local pressure, Washington ordered that the Apaches should be consolidated at the San Carlos Reservation, which would soon become known as Fort Apache. The move not only brought the people together, but competing leaders as well, and before long a power struggle turned San Carlos into a battlefield. Soon the Apaches began to drift away and the war broke out all over again. After his second campaign Crook stood up and took credit for another major victory, but although his soldiers had killed hundreds of Apaches, the leaders were at large and angry. Some of the most rebellious of them were still at the Warm Springs Reservation waiting for transfer to San Carlos, and the surrounding countryside was filled with warriors waiting for an opportunity to strike. Among them was the Mimbres Apache chieftain Victorio, who was regarded as the fiercest of all Apaches. When he finally surrendered, he was held prisoner at Warm Springs out of fear that his presence among his old followers, and not a few old enemies, would surely result in an uprising. He was held there for a year before the government, in a cost-cutting move, decided to move him and his people to San Carlos, but Victorio escaped before the move could be made. He eventually surrendered, but escaped again, along with one hundred and fifty Mescalero warriors, when he discovered that he had been tried *in absentia* and found guilty in the white man's court on charges of murder.

The trail of dead they left behind led straight in the direction of Mexico, which prompted the government to send in fresh troops to pursue the renegades and capture Victorio and the other Apache leaders in the bargain. A thousand soldiers, plus scores of Indian scouts and interested local citizens, took up the chase, and although there were a few skirmishes, Victorio finally reached the safety of Mexico and when the pursuers arrived at the border, they were turned back by local authorities. As it happened, the Mexican government had offered a huge reward for Victorio's head, and several weeks later it was collected by Mexican soldiers. By October 1880 Victorio was dead, and so were sixty of his warriors, but the rest escaped, including a grizzled, eighty-year-old chief named Nana, who led the survivors northward on a six-week reign of terror more frightening than any the white men had yet seen. He finally retreated into Mexico to fight another day. Although Nana was old and sick – he couldn't mount a horse without difficulty – in less than two months he led his warriors over a thousand miles of enemy country, living off the land as they went. He fought eight pitched battles with the horse soldiers and won all of them with no losses on his side. At its height, his little band was never bigger than forty men, and through most of his campaign he had only fifteen. He was pursued by more than a thousand soldiers helped by some four hundred civilians and he managed to frustrate them all.

The raiding and the counterattacks continued for months until General Crook decided to take the war directly to the Apache sanctuaries across the Mexican border. No agreement between the two governments made the move legal, but taking his best men with him Crook crossed into Mexico with the kind of stealth that would make an Apache proud of him. Then he vanished from public view. After ten days of hard marching, during which they found signs of Apaches but none in the flesh, Crook's scouts led him to what they said was the Chiricahua stronghold, but it was abandoned. Taking it for his own camp, the General sent out scouting parties and within four days one of them made contact with the enemy. Among the captives taken in the brief battle was a squaw who agreed to bring another famous Apache leader, Geronimo, and his lieutenants for a peace parley. After a day of discussion, the chief still wasn't sure it was wise to surrender, and Crook told him to go back to his camp and think it over. He also allowed him to keep his weapons, and that tipped the balance. The following day Geronimo surrendered, and within a few more days the other Apache leaders in Mexico followed his lead. All of them and their followers were removed to Fort Apache, but Geronimo had been given permission to stay in Mexico until all his people were rounded up, and six months later he had still not appeared at the reservation. Another three months passed before he showed up, and his excuse was that he had used the time to steal gifts for his relatives and friends with a few raids on Mexican rancheros. Eventually reservation life began to bore Geronimo and he escaped back into Mexico with forty-two warriors and ninety-two squaws. A troop of U.S. Cavalry and several companies of Indian scouts followed close behind. It took several weeks to track down the escapees. It might have taken longer but the hunted found the hunters and Geronimo called for surrender terms. He finally agreed to stop fighting and to allow himself to be deported to a reservation in Florida if the whites would promise to return him to Fort Apache after two years. Just short of the border, Geronimo and some of his men got drunk and, deciding that they were marching into a trap, turned and escaped back into the hills. The others kept going north and were soon on a train headed for Florida. Meanwhile, a new force of five thousand soldiers joined with the Mexican army scouring the hills of Mexico for Geronimo and the twenty-two warriors and fourteen women and children who had escaped with him. Five months later the rebels surrendered, and on September 8, 1886, Geronimo and his people left their homeland for the concentration camp in Florida. Some seven hundred Apaches made the trip, but rather than the promised two years of imprisonment they were held there for three, and then were transferred to Alabama. A few years later, the three hundred survivors were moved again to Fort Sill, Oklahoma, and in 1913 the two hundred and fifty that were left were finally reunited with their people at the Mescalero Reservation in New Mexico. They had come home, but the land was no longer theirs.

In Arizona and New Mexico Native Americans didn't become full citizens of the United States until 1948, and since then large numbers of them have assimilated into the general population. But many still live on the old reservations, including the Navajo, whose lands extend over Utah, Arizona and New Mexico. Some 142,238 of Arizona's 203,527 Indians – the Navajo, Apache, O'odham, Hopi, Yavapai and others – live on reservations. Of New Mexico's 134,355 Pueblo, Apache, and Navajo Indians, 87,659 live on reservations and Indian trust lands. In Utah 8,577 of the state's 24,283 Utes, Navajos, and other tribes live on reservations and Indian trust lands. The total Native American population is almost two million, but nowhere in the United States do they live as much in the ways of their ancestors as in the Southwest. It is a way of life their ancestors fought hard to preserve – no matter which side of the story you choose to believe.

Like a letter from the ancient past, the pyramid called El Castillo (the Castle) (previous page) at Chichén Itzá on Mexico's Yucatan Peninsula reveals the mathematical and astronomical brilliance of the early Mayans. Mayan legends claim that the Pyramid of the Soothsayer, El Pirámide del Adivíno, at Uxmal (facing page bottom) was constructed in a single day; archaeologists say it took three centuries. Aztec Indian traditions survive in Ballet Folklorico dances (facing page top) and rituals like the blowing of the sacred conch horn (above).

A millennium ago, Anasazi Indians lived throughout southern Utah. In what is now Natural Bridges National Monument they planted corn and beans among the natural sandstone bridges (above) and used stones, mud, and wood to construct homes beneath protective overhangs in the canyon wall (facing page top). In what is now Capitol Reef National Park (facing page bottom), they hunted, farmed, and prayed that the clouds would bring rain to fill the dry streambeds.

Much about the Anasazi baffles anthropologists. Did they build the mysterious square towers (above) at Hovenweep National Monument in southeastern Utah to observe the stars? To communicate with distant villages? To watch for enemies? What do figures like those (facing page top) they pecked into the sandstone at Utah's Capitol Reef National Park symbolize? And what influences, beginning about AD 700, helped them to improve on their simple underground pit houses like those (facing page bottom) at Anasazi State Park in southern Utah and build their homes above ground? Most puzzling of all, why did they abandon their dramatic landscapes in southern Utah (overleaf) and elsewhere around AD 1300?

At Mesa Verde National Park in southwestern Colorado the Anasazi built elaborate stone villages like the compact Far View ruin (facing page bottom) on the mesa top, where they could farm and collect rainwater easily. But around AD 1100 they also began constructing dwellings like the 114-room Spruce Tree House (facing page top) in the cliffsides, presumably for greater protection from their enemies. At Cliff Palace (above and overleaf), they lived, ground corn, and conducted ceremonial rituals in a nearly impregnable complex that included 220 rooms and 23 kivas.

When Anglo-American settlers moved into northwest New Mexico in the 1870s, they encountered Anasazi ruins and decided, incorrectly, that the Aztecs had built them. Now known as Aztec Ruins National Monument, this 500-room Anasazi complex features a superb great kiva (below, bottom, and facing page bottom), built about AD 1100. The angle of the sunlight passing through wall openings of the circular ceremonial chamber may have helped medicine people calculate the equinoxes. Fine astronomers, the Anasazi used a natural rock formation at the top of La Fajada Butte (right) at nearby Chaco Culture National Historical Park to determine the arrival of the winter solstice.

Dozens of small, circular chambers (above) at Pueblo Bonito in Chaco Culture National Historical Park probably served as kivas for families or clans. Skilled masons, the Chacoans built the thick walls of Kin Kletso (facing page top) by pouring a core of rubble between outer walls of cut sandstone. During excavation of Chetro Ketl (facing page bottom) archaeologists found more than 17,000 stone and shell beads in niches concealed in the stone walls. Seen from the mesatop above Chaco Canyon (overleaf) Pueblo Bonito, the largest of the canyon's villages, lies like a half-moon along the canyon floor.

According to Navajo tradition, Navajos arrived in the Southwest in time to observe the rise and fall of the Anasazi. The Anasazi's mistake, the Navajos believe, was that they settled in towns. When the urban Anasazi disappeared, the rural Navajos survived, and numerous Anasazi ruins dot Navajo territory today. At Navajo National Monument (right) in Arizona, Navajos named these ruins Betatakin, a Navajo word meaning "ledge house." At Canyon de Chelly National Monument (overleaf), also in Arizona, Navajos still live in the valley below White House ruin, which the Anasazi built about AD 1000 and abandoned about three hundred years later.

At Wupatki National Monument in Arizona early Indians built their stone homes on a waterless plain, earning them the name Sinagua (Without Water). Some anthropologists consider the Sinagua a branch of the Anasazi. The monument's largest ruins, Wupatki (above), probably housed 125 people at its peak, about AD 1200. The much smaller Lomaki ruins (facing page top) lie close to an unusual geological formation known as an earth crack, a vertical fissure in the underlying limestone. The Sinagua probably considered it a sacred site. Hopi Indian tradition maintains their ancestors lived at Wukoki ruins (facing page bottom) and other monument sites.

At Tuzigoot National Monument (these pages) in central Arizona, Sinagua Indians built a stone village on a ridge overlooking the Verde River Valley. For three centuries they farmed the surrounding lowlands; by AD 1400 they had disappeared. Anglo-American settlers in the 1800s named the ruins at nearby Montezuma Castle National Monument (overleaf) after Aztec emperor Montezuma because they believed Aztecs had built them. In fact, Sinagua Indians constructed the stone fortress in a natural alcove in the cliffside and shared their precious water supplies with nearby Hohokam Indians, some of whom continued to live in pit houses.

In 1540 Spanish explorer Francisco Vásquez de Coronado found Pueblo Indians, the descendants of the Anasazi, living in central New Mexico. He spent that winter along the Río Grande in a Pueblo Indian village like the one at Coronado State Monument (facing page top), where an ancient mural depicts the elements of Pueblo Indian life. At Pecos Pueblo (facing page bottom), Coronado and his men met the man they called El Turco, the Turk, a Plains Indian who led them farther east in search of the gold-filled land of Quivira. Coronado failed to find gold, and eventually a Pueblo Indian village in central New Mexico (above) acquired the name Gran Quivira.

Apart from their ruins, the most striking physical legacy of the Southwest's early Indians are the pictorial writings, called petroglyphs, that they left on the rocks. At Painted Rocks State Park (above) in Arizona, symbols hint at stories about the interconnectedness of animals and human beings. At Comanche Gap (facing page top) in the Galisteo Basin of New Mexico the figure of Kokopelli, the hunch-backed flute player, links the pre- and post-conquest Pueblo peoples of New Mexico with the Hopi Indians of Arizona. At Chevelon Creek, in Arizona, Hopis say a female figure carved in the rocks (facing page bottom) depicts a kachina spirit giving birth to humankind.

Anthropologists believe that when the Anasazi abandoned their homes around AD 1300, many of them moved to the Río Grande area of central and northern New Mexico. Tribal legends at Taos Pueblo (right) support this viewpoint. When the Spanish arrived, colonial officials developed laws to forbid settlers from building too close to Indian villages, but the two cultures mingled. They still do. Photography is prohibited in the interior of the Pueblo church shown here, but visitors find native symbols like the sun, moon, and stalks of corn painted on the wall behind the Christian altar. And ancient, pre-Christian rituals often precede and follow the Catholic mass.

The Pueblo peoples also borrowed cultural elements from non-Pueblo Indians. Like some other Pueblo tribes, Taos Indians (left, below and facing page) wear Plains Indian ceremonial attire to dance the Comanche dance. Many ancient Anasazi customs still mark contemporary Pueblo Indian life, however, including the division of villagers into Summer People and Winter People. At Taos Pueblo, the Taos River (bottom), symbolizes that division as it separates the village into two parts.

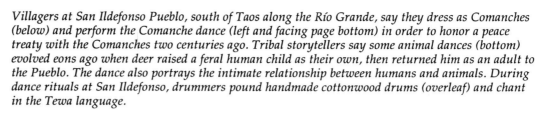

Villagers at San Ildefonso Pueblo, south of Taos along the Río Grande, say they dress as Comanches (below) and perform the Comanche dance (left and facing page bottom) in order to honor a peace treaty with the Comanches two centuries ago. Tribal storytellers say some animal dances (bottom) evolved eons ago when deer raised a feral human child as their own, then returned him as an adult to the Pueblo. The dance also portrays the intimate relationship between humans and animals. During dance rituals at San Ildefonso, drummers pound handmade cottonwood drums (overleaf) and chant in the Tewa language.

59

On San Ildefonso's feast day, January 23, dancers prance like game animals (top) on one plaza while dancers on a different plaza yip and howl like coyotes in the Comanche dance (above). Non-sacred dances like the Comanche dance may be performed year round. Sacred dances have traditionally been tied to moieties and performed seasonally. The animal dances date to the days when deer and other game animals provided villagers with their winter food. The basket dance (facing page) honors planting time, summer, and harvest.

For centuries, buffalo herds grazed on the plains
east of the Río Grande. Pueblo Indians traveled
out to hunt them; today the buffalo dance (right)
is their most widely performed animal dance.
Here, dancers from San Ildefonso Pueblo reenact
the ancient ritual, in which a woman known as
the Buffalo Mother symbolizes the mother of all
large animals. In Pueblo legends, the Buffalo
Mother appears to young men during their vision
quests. She offers them a task and gives them three
days to perform it. In one legend she sends a
young man out to search for the answer to the
question, "What do women really want?" The
answer, he discovers, is, "The freedom to be true
to themselves."

When winter temperatures fall below freezing, Pueblo men may wear blankets around their waists like kilts (below) or over their shoulders like shawls (facing page bottom). On San Ildefonso's feast day (right) blanketed drummers stand waiting for dancers to emerge from the kiva. From the outside, many Pueblo Indian kivas today resemble ordinary adobe rooms; many are angular rather than circular and above ground rather than subterranean. But the rituals performed inside them still link the Pueblos to their Anasazi ancestors.

When Don Juan de Oñate and his settlers reached northern New Mexico in 1598, they settled near present-day San Juan Pueblo (above). Today San Juan serves as a center for the eight northern Pueblo tribes. Like other Pueblo Indians, the people of San Juan perform the Comanche dance (facing page and above) and the corn dance (top). Centuries of interaction with outsiders has taught the Pueblo peoples not to share their world view with outsiders. Much of what we know today about Pueblo ceremonial life comes from the writings of a San Juan Pueblo Indian, anthropologist Alfonso Ortiz.

At Santa Clara Pueblo, between San Juan Pueblo and San Ildefonso Pueblo along the upper Río Grande, the women wear painted headdresses called tablitas when they perform the corn dance (these pages and overleaf). Colors and designs on the tablitas symbolize important elements of Pueblo life: the sun, the sky, rain, kiva steps, clouds, kachina spirits, and mountains.

When the Spanish arrived in the New World, they brought with them a dance tradition which is said to date back to the days when the Moors invaded Spain: the Matachines dance. In Mexico, the Aztecs, Tarahumaras, and other Indians adopted the dance. In New Mexico it survives in places like Santa Clara Pueblo (these pages), where villagers add feathers to their headdresses and beat Indian drums. A young girl (facing page bottom) plays La Malinche, a controversial Indian woman who aided Cortés in the conquest of Mexico. In northern New Mexico La Malinche symbolizes innocence and purity.

In some Pueblo groups, Winter People are called Turquoise People. The turquoise paint on the bannister that leads into this kiva at Santa Clara Pueblo (below) links the kiva to the Winter People. Jémez Pueblo (right) lies west of the Río Grande and is the only place where the Towa language survives. At Pojoaqué Pueblo (facing page bottom) and at other Pueblo villages, even young children participate in dance ceremonies. The mesatop village at Acoma Pueblo (overleaf) vies with Taos Pueblo for the title of most picturesque.

All nineteen Pueblo Indian tribes in New Mexico retain their ancient languages. Of the five surviving languages – Tewa, Tiwa, Towa, Keresan, and Zuni – Tewa, Tiwa, and Towa show a clear relationship to the Nahuatl language of the Aztecs. Keresan, spoken by the Acoma Indians and five other Pueblo tribes, puzzles linguists. So does the Zuni language. Culturally, the people of Zuni Pueblo show close connections to other Pueblo tribes. Their costumes in rituals like the turkey dance (facing page), rainbow dance (above), and olla dance (top) reflect common Pueblo themes.

When Coronado arrived at Zuni Pueblo in 1540, he found the residents living in six separate villages. Today Zuni remains the largest Pueblo group in New Mexico, more than 7,000 strong. It also remains devoted to tradition. When young people dance the turkey dance (facing page), they know that the sashes they wear represent falling rain, and the gourd rattles they shake imitate its sound. They know that women dance in a shuffle-like step to reflect their closeness to Mother Earth. They know the massive turquoise jewelry worn by the elders (above) reflects their affinity to Father Sky.

Stark buttes and dry plains mark the Arizona homeland of the Hopi Indians. For centuries the Hopis
have practiced dry-land farming techniques; in 1870 a leader named Tuba established the farming
settlement of Moenkopi (left). Today, five Indian tribes live in or near the Grand Canyon of the
Colorado River in Arizona: Navajo, Havasupai, Paiute, Hualapai, and Hopi. At the Desert View
lookout (above) architectural designer Mary Elizabeth Jane Colter designed a stone watchtower in
the 1920s to resemble the towers of the Anasazi, who built homes at more than 500 sites around the
canyon. The interior of the tower is sometimes called Hopi House.

Hopi artist Fred Kabotie painted scenes from Hopi legends on the walls of Hopi House at the Grand Canyon. With the staircase buttes of the Grand Canyon visible through the window (right), visitors encounter ancient symbols representing the sun, the moon, garden plots, and the kivas in which the sacred spirits live. A large circular painting (overleaf), tells the story of the young man who became the first human being to navigate the Colorado River. He searches for the Snake people, who alone know the secret of making rain. The Snake priest reveals the secret and marries his daughter to the traveler, and the couple return to Hopi land.

To arrange her hair in traditional Hopi fashion, a young woman (below) parts it in a careful zigzag and wraps it around cardboard forms. Images of kachinas often decorate traditional Hopi headdresses (left). Supernatural beings, kachinas mediate between humans and the gods. The carved kachinas shown here, often called kachina dolls, were made by artists Elsie and Stacy Talahytewa (bottom), Les David (facing page top), Bert Nahsonhoya (facing page bottom left) and Godfrey Hayah (facing page bottom right).

Famous for their brilliance as guerrilla fighters, the Apache Indians preserve elaborate ritual traditions related to those of their linguistic and cultural cousins, the Navajos. Like other indigenous Southwest peoples, they retain traditional dress (these pages) from earlier eras for ceremonial events. The crosses come from pre-Christian symbolism; sixteenth-century explorers in the Southwest reported meeting non-Pueblo peoples, probably Apaches, who wore crosses painted on their heads. Today the scenic wildness of the Salt River Canyon (overleaf) on Apache land in eastern Arizona makes tourism a major source of income for the White Mountain Apaches.

In "Heading Home" (facing page bottom), "Dineh" (above), and other sculptures, Chiricahua Apache sculptor Allan Houser depicts traditional Apache and Navajo motifs. In 1992 the top-selling artist received the National Medal of Arts, the nation's highest honor in the visual and performing arts. As an adolescent, Houser's father fought with Geronimo. After the long years of Chiricahua Apache incarceration in Florida and Oklahoma, the artist, who was born in 1914, became the first member of his tribe to be born a free man again. Houser's son Bob, also an artist, uses the Apache spelling of the family name, Haozous. In sculpting his steel "Bear with Planes with Clouds with Fish" (facing page top), Haozous combines traditional and contemporary themes.

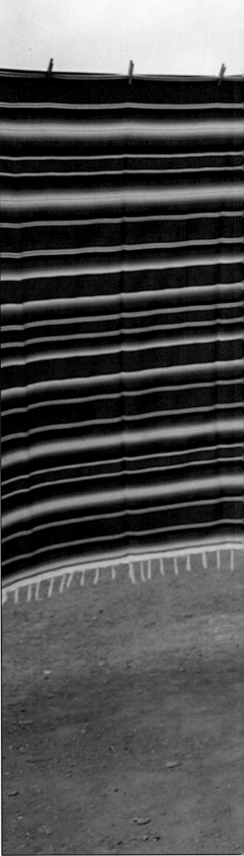

In the blue sky over the Indian country of eastern Arizona (top left), a frayed U.S. flag bears the image of an Indian. Peace pipe in hand, the figure symbolizes Indians throughout American history who wanted only peace with their neighbors, not war. Along the interstate in eastern Arizona, many gift shops display stylized designs, like this dancing kachina (bottom left), based on Indian legends and art. Beside the highway near the east entrance to the Grand Canyon, Navajo vendors sell blankets (above) woven in Mexico in Southwest Indian motifs.

In Gallup, New Mexico, the trading post tradition survives in stores that cater to both Indian and non-Indian customers. At Tobe Turpen's (left), Hopi kachina dolls, Navajo weavings, and Zuni jewelry fill display cases. At Richardson Trading Company, in one part of the store Navajos and other Indians gather at a counter (facing page bottom) to trade pottery and other items for cash, while a display of fine Navajo weavings and Navajo dolls (below) in another part of the store appeals to tourists and other non-Indian buyers.

Arizona's Petrified Forest National Park (facing page top) contains many sites sacred to Navajos and other local tribes. Similarly, the Painted Desert and the Little Painted Desert (facing page bottom) remain sacred. Navajo tribal myths explain the origins of landscapes such as northwestern New Mexico's stark Bisti Wilderness (above), which takes its name from a Navajo word meaning badlands. Probably no part of Navajo country is better known to outsiders than Monument Valley (overleaf), on the border between Utah and Arizona. There native horses roam free, and old women tell their grandchildren the Navajo version of history: "No matter what you read in books, the truth is that Navajos have always had horses and sheep."

103

When Navajo women perform the basket dance (above), the coiled baskets they hold in their hands link them to a basketmaking tradition in the Southwest which dates back more than two thousand years. In ceremonials that began hundreds of years ago, Navajos make temporary paintings, commonly called sand paintings (facing page top right) from colored sand, bits of charcoal, pollen, and other natural materials. In a modern variation on that theme, Navajo artisans use glue and backing boards (facing page bottom) to make sand paintings for sale to tourists. In the limited-edition bronze sculpture "Prayer for Mother Earth," (facing page top left) prize-winning Navajo sculptor Larry Yazzie expresses a contemporary concern for the future of Mother Earth.

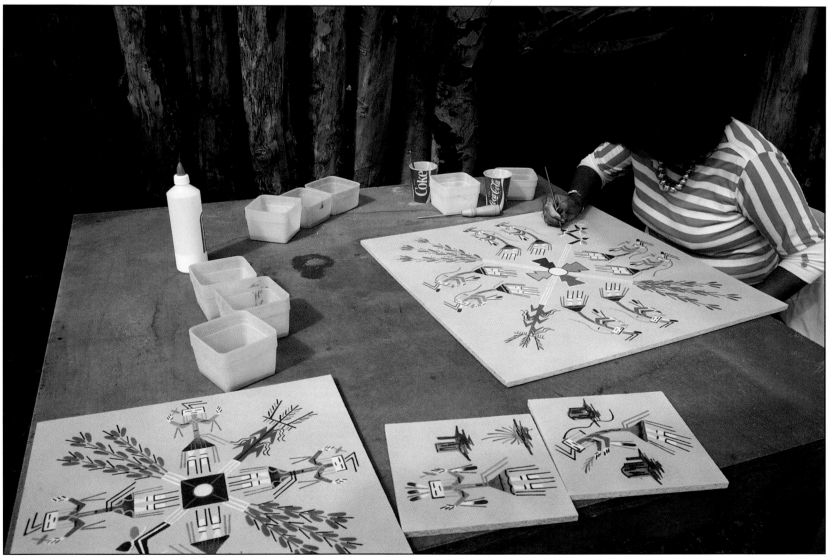

Navajo artist Johnson Antonio carves Navajo figures from cottonwood (facing page). For paint he uses watercolors and dleesh, a clay which Navajos apply to their bodies before ceremonials. Navajos are known worldwide for their fine silversmithing. Popular items include concha belts (top) and bracelets of turquoise and silver (above). A family's wealth may be measured in its silver jewelry, which can be pawned at trading posts to provide quick cash.

*Navajos call the volcanic formation known in English as Shiprock (facing page top) Tse-Bida'hi,
"The Rock with Wings." According to one legend, Tse-Bida'hi was once a giant bird that carried the
Navajos to the Southwest on its back from the land beyond the setting summer sun. For centuries
after their arrival, Navajos hid from enemies like the Utes in a labyrinth of canyons and rocks in
northeastern Arizona known as Canyon de Chelly (facing page bottom). Among the natural wonders
on the sparsely-populated Navajo reservation are the Grand Falls of the Little Colorado River (above).*

Of all the Indian tribes of the Southwest, none live in a more remote location than the Havasupai. After driving nearly 100 miles from the nearest town, visitors and villagers alike must walk or ride burros or horses for the final ten miles. The trail begins on a high bluff (right) and drops down a series of steep switchbacks into the canyon. From there it follows dry stream beds until it arrives at the village of Supai (overleaf) in Cataract Canyon, a side canyon of the Grand Canyon.

From about 300 BC to AD 1150 the Anasazi Indians lived in Nevada's Valley of Fire (facing page top and bottom), in a wonderland of sculpted sandstone where summer temperatures reach 120 degrees Fahrenheit. Farther north, Indians have lived among the rocks and caves that surround Nevada's Pyramid Lake (above) and its predecessor, Lake Lahontan, for at least 10,000 years. Today the lake belongs to Paiute Indians, who speak one of the many Southwest Indian tongues that are related to the Nahuatl language of the Aztecs.

Between 1880 and 1926, hundreds of Yaqui Indians moved north from the state of Sonora, Mexico, and settled in southern Arizona. Today their descendants retain such Mexican Indian traditions as the Baile de los Viejitos, "Dance of the Little Old Men" (right), which dates back to pre-Conquest days. On the feast day of Nuestra Señora de Guadalupe, December 12, Yaqui residents of the village of Guadalupe, a suburb of Phoenix, play the drum (below) and dance in honor of Our Lady of Guadalupe. At the late artist Ted De Grazia's Gallery in the Sun in Tucson, wall paintings at a chapel of Our Lady of Guadalupe include a Yaqui deer dancer (facing page bottom).

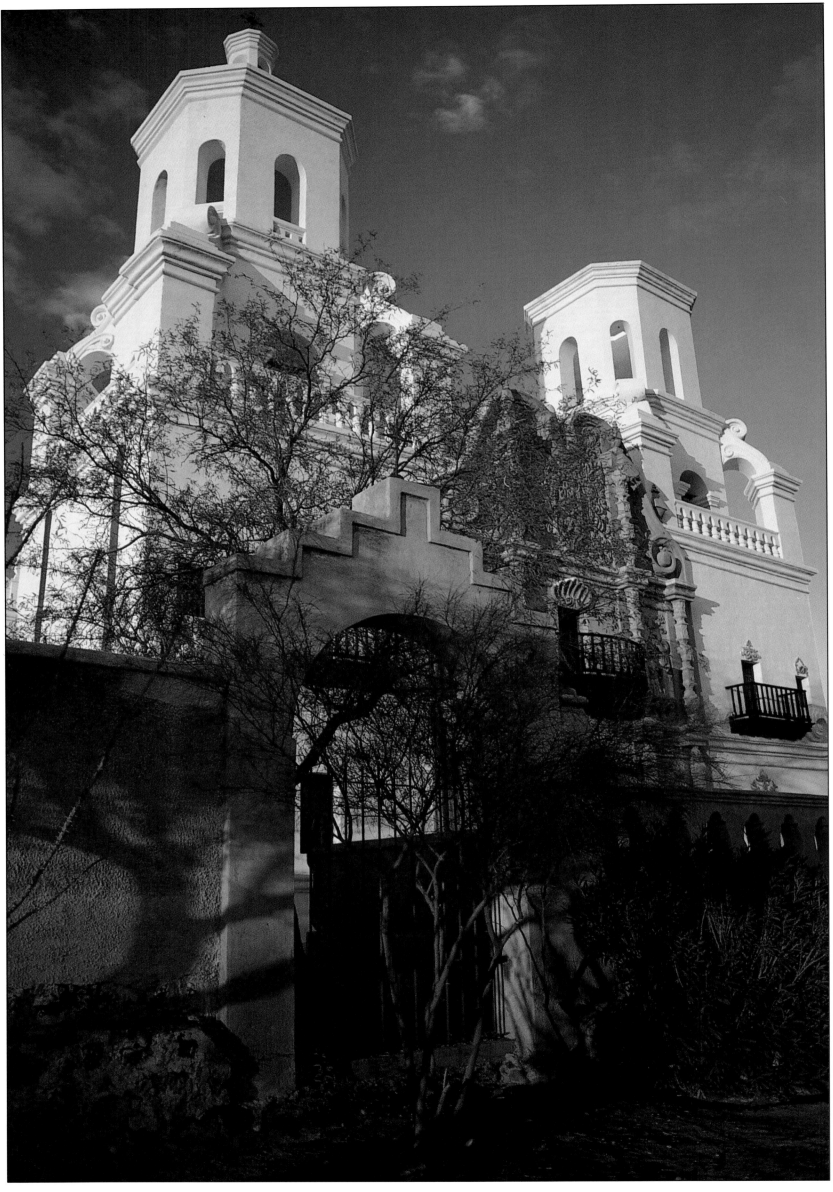

Formerly known as Papagos, the O'odham Indians of southern Arizona probably descend from the ancient Hohokam. South of Tucson, their 200-year-old church, San Xavier del Bac (facing page), is considered the most beautiful mission church in the Southwest. In December, O'odham Indians participate in the reenactment of the legend of Our Lady of Guadalupe, in which the Virgin Mary appeared to a poor Indian boy, Juan Diego. As a sign, she caused an image of herself to appear on his tilma (above). In a country of desert lowlands dotted with mountains (overleaf), the O'odham people have thrived by adapting to their environment.

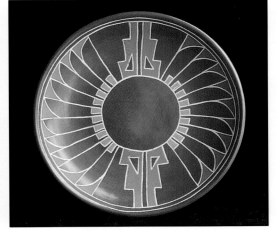

At the annual Indian Market in Santa Fe, New Mexico, thousands of collectors gather (facing page bottom) to buy Indian arts and crafts. Kiowa Indians arrive with buckskin costumes (facing page top left) and dream shields (facing page top right). Vendors sell pottery like these pieces by Lorencita Pino of Tesuque Pueblo (above left), Anita Suazo of Santa Clara Pueblo (above center), and Dale Sanchez of Acoma Pueblo (above right). At some Santa Fe events, Pueblo Indian dancers invite non-Indians to join them (top). Many Santa Fe shops specialize in Indian jewelry like the turquoise and silver concha belts at Packard's (overleaf). Sometimes crafts like these ojos de dios (following page) combine Hispanic and Indian themes.

INDEX